1. *Change in the landscape: harvesting timber.*

FORESTRY IN SCOTLAND

A POLICY PAPER

COUNTRYSIDE COMMISSION FOR SCOTLAND

4

CONTENTS

DESIGNED AND PUBLISHED BY THE
COUNTRYSIDE COMMISSION FOR SCOTLAND
Battleby, Redgorton, Perth, PH1 3EW

Printed in Scotland by Holmes McDougall Limited, Edinburgh

Acknowledgements
Grateful thanks are due to The Forestry Commission for photographs 3a, 6, 8, 11, and 24a, b, c, d, T. Huxley 20, R. Fairley 12, 16, 25 and 26, W Forbes 15 and L Gill all the remainder.

FOREWORD

From my life long interest in the sensible use of the countryside, it has given me as much satisfaction that the Commission has developed its own balanced policies on forestry in Scotland, as it has given me pleasure to have been directly involved in seeing this task to its completion, in this publication.

This personal observation is made as a reminder that however much policy statements are couched in an impersonal style, ultimately they reflect the collective views of a number of individuals; in this instance myself and my fellow Commissioners, appointed by the Secretary of State for Scotland, and our staff. We have, of course, consulted widely (a complete list is given in Appendix I) and we have given careful consideration to all the observations made to us in response to our discussion paper first issued in November 1985. Nevertheless, the final outcome is our view: a policy statement by the Countryside Commission for Scotland, and we do not perceive it as being allied to any particular lobby, whether that lobby be seen by others as 'forestry', 'conservation' or any other land use interest.

Rather, foremost in our thoughts we have seen a need to set out policies which we believe as being right for Scotland in such a way as to arrive at what we see as being a correct balance, in the circumstances prevailing today, for each of a range of issues. In the future, circumstances will change and the weight of argument then prevailing may lead the Commission to arrive at a different assessment of balance and different policies.

Indeed, in some particular matters, we recognise that developments will move forward quite quickly and that even in as little as a year from now some of our statements will be overtaken by events. For the most part, however, we hope that this publication will have lasting value and that where it becomes outdated, this will be because our recommendations have made positive contributions for the benefit of Scotland.

J Roger Carr
Chairman

Battleby, Redgorton,
PERTH   5 May 1986

1 INTRODUCTION

1.1   The Countryside Commission for Scotland has two main functions:
 (i) the provision, development and improvement of facilities for the enjoyment of the Scottish countryside, and
 (ii) the conservation and enhancement of its natural beauty and amenity.

1.2   In carrying out these functions, we are required to have regard for the balanced socio-economic development of the countryside. This requirement was written into our enabling legislation 20 years ago as an encouragement to adopt policies which took account of people who live and work in the Scottish countryside. That need is just as great today. Policies about the way land is used must not be measured solely in terms of the products and profits accruing from use of land. The effect of policies on rural employment and the development of opportunities for people who earn their living in the countryside to enjoy that way of life to the full must also be taken into account. In terms of our responsibilities, we do so not only because this is supportive of a general good, but also because an attractive countryside and enjoyment of it is crucially dependent on the maintenance of a healthy rural population.

1.3   This socio-economic need is reflected in our attitude towards forestry. We recognise that successive Governments have strongly supported forestry and encouraged afforestation of suitable land, not only in order to reduce Britain's dependence on overseas supplies of timber and wood products by producing raw material for industry, but also to provide opportunities for employment in rural areas where jobs are scarce. Great Britain remains poorly wooded by comparison with the European Community neighbours despite substantial new planting and restocking programmes over the last 60 years. In 1983 it was only 9% self-sufficient in timber products against an EEC average of 33%. Even Scotland, the most heavily wooded part of Britain, has only 13% of its land under trees, despite substantial increases in the area devoted to forestry.

1.4   Nevertheless, forestry is currently the subject of much public debate. Although many people accept forestry, including the new post-war forests, as an acceptable part of the Scottish landscape, many others do not. They see forestry, in particular afforestation and the almost exclusive use of coniferous species, as damaging to the appearance of familiar, well-loved countryside and as seriously diminishing the nature conservation interests of the land. They consider that there is a lack of public control over the major changes which afforestation can bring to the countryside and they regard the tax arrangements for forestry as unfairly fostering private interests to the detriment of a wider public good, notwithstanding that these arrangements have been accepted by successive Governments as an appropriate means of support for forestry in a way which takes account of its long time-cycle of investment.

1.5   The Countryside Commission for Scotland recognises that most additional afforestation in Britain is going to take place in Scotland and at a faster pace than in other parts of the country, and that this will be done mostly by the private sector with grant-aid and support by way of fiscal reliefs. Thus forestry will be a major cause for change in the appearance of the Scottish countryside and, in carrying out our review function, we have examined a range of matters relating to forestry and are publishing this policy statement as the result of these deliberations.

1.6   Over the past two years, however, and especially in the last six months, debate about forestry has become closely involved in debate about other land uses, especially agriculture. The reasons for this have been well rehearsed in recent reports and conferences and in Appendix 2 we have assembled annotated lists of seminars, conferences, reports and review groups known to us, which we hope may act as a helpful reminder of the wealth of ideas which the current debate about land use is generating and which the Commission has sought to take into account in preparing a policy on forestry.

2. A mixture of land use: agriculture and forestry.

1.7   Indeed, standing back from consideration of detailed matters relating to any particular land use, the overwhelming conclusion points to the need for everyone to adopt a more comprehensive and less sectional approach to the future of land use in Scotland. Although today this should be so self-obvious as not to require stating, the point has to be made in this paper focusing on a particular land use, lest anyone conclude that in addressing our minds to forestry policy we have overlooked this important land use scene.

1.8   Finally in this Introduction, we acknowledge with gratitude the carefully considered and constructive observations provided in response to our discussion paper, first issued in November. The fact that so many people have welcomed our general approach to the subject has been gratifying, not just because this is a cause for self-congratulation, but because it appears to us to be an optimistic pointer for the future, that commonly agreed policies are an achievable objective.

3. The role of forestry in rural
    employment.

(a) Ditching, prior to afforestation.

(b) Dunkeld Sawmills.

2 GENERAL CONSIDERATIONS

2.1   The history of Scotland's extensive natural tree cover and deforestation due to man stretches back for centuries and, compared to many other types of land use, the operational timescale of forestry is long. Even for short rotation forestry in areas subject to severe wind-throw, 30 to 40 years is an expected minimum period from planting to harvesting and a second rotation may be under consideration even while the first is still young, while for some broad-leaved species, rotations may be well over 100 years. Where the focus of interest shifts from timber production, especially in the case of woodlands of interest for nature conservation, amenity, recreation and sport, the timescale may be even longer.

2.2   Against this long timescale inherent in the biology of trees, there is the much shorter timescale for afforestation to make an impact. For previously unplanted land the evidence of afforestation — fencing, hill roads and deep ploughing — can bring about substantial visual change in as little as one year. Within a decade new forests can transform a countryside environment long before people's collective memory of what the landscape was like before afforestation has become overlain by familiarity with the new. For purposes of recreation, especially access to hills and mountains, the sense of displeasure may last a lifetime and recollections of youthful freedoms to roam anywhere across open moorland, remain undiminished, even by well signed forest trails. Young forests, especially, whether broadleaved or conifer, are less visually attractive than older forests, although much can be done to make them attractive by good design.

2.3   Thus there is still vocal and widespread criticism of Britain's new forests and continued use is made of the pejorative term 'blanket afforestation'. Nevertheless, the fact that the public do value forests for recreation is evident from the Forestry Commission's estimate of 6-8 million day visits to its forests in Scotland each year, despite there being ample alternative countryside for recreation.

2.4   We recognise that the landscape of Scotland owes much of its appearance today to the effects of man over the centuries and that the countryside is constantly subject to change. Indeed, change *per se* is an inherent characteristic of the countryside which should as often be welcomed as resisted. In relation to landscape, we prefer the term 'conservation' to 'preservation' because conservation — defined as the wise use of resources — allows for change, whereas preservation implies holding to the *status quo*. Of itself, the word 'conservation' can refer to anything requiring to be conserved and, therefore, wherever we intend it to refer to landscape or nature conservation, we have included the appropriate qualification. Unfortunately, in much public debate about the environment, conservation is often not so qualified and much misunderstanding can on occasion be created by an implication that all facets of a case for conservation are facing in the same direction.

2.5   In the long timescale of forestry, we consider that the present pace of change from unplanted land is likely to diminish significantly by the end of the century or in the early years of the next century because, by then, most land that is ever in practice going to become available for planting in Scotland will probably have been planted. Thus in the medium timescale of the second half of this century, we recognise that Scotland is probably moving through the concluding years of a transition period in the expansion of forestry, towards a new and more stable period of rotational forest management in the 21st century.

3 HOW MUCH MORE AFFORESTATION?

3.1 Although speculating about future land use is hazardous, some reasoned guesswork is possible. A starting point is to consider what finite limit there may be to the amount of land theoretically suitable for planting. In 1976, taking physical and economic constraints into account, the Forestry Commission estimated this to be about a third of Scotland's land area, ie about 30%. Today this limit may be thought to have increased because of the effect of the current revision of agricultural structures and the recently announced review by the Department of Agriculture and Fisheries for Scotland of their policy in regard to releasing land from agriculture to forestry. Nevertheless, a theoretical limit still exists, even if it is somewhat more than the figure of 30% already quoted. Against this theoretical limit, it is known that the present extent of land under trees in Scotland is 13%.

3.2 The question then arises: by how much will the actual extent of land under trees increase between a theoretical maximum of about 30% or more and the present overall average of 13%? It is generally agreed that the actual extent of land ever likely to be planted will be significantly less than the theoretical limit, however that notional figure is estimated, because constraints will increasingly come into force long before that level is reached. Many of these constraints exist already, for example land used for water catchment, nature conservation, agriculture and sporting. Whether these constraints alter in future is not so important as their collective effect in limiting the continued spread of forestry. So how does one project forward a possible answer to the question about the overall percentage of the area at which further extension of the present land under trees in Scotland will largely cease?

3.3 A possible answer is to project forward the current rate of new planting, of the order of 20,000 hectares per annum, which area equates with about 0.25% of the land area of Scotland. If this expansion continues at about the same rate to the end of the century, the result would be about 4% more land under trees, bringing the overall Scottish average to 17%. What will actually happen cannot, of course, be predicted with certainty. It is worth recording that the current annual total planting, including restocking, would sustain a forest of only 1.4 million hectares (18% of the land area) assuming an average 60 year rotation. The possibility exists, of course, of a greater rate of new planting and longer rotations. For example, it is now commonly forecast that one consequence of agricultural surpluses will be an increase in the amount of land going to forestry.

3.4 The point of such speculation, however, does not lie in the accuracy of the forecast but rather that, even if the increased overall average is significantly more than 4%, say twice that amount, ie 8%, it should help to forestall more extreme concerns that 'blanket afforestation' will soon cover most of Scotland. So long as the annual rate of new planting continues much as at present, by the beginning of the 21st century, Scotland as a whole will still be significantly less forested than many countries of mainland Europe, for example France (27%) or the Federal Republic of Germany (30%).

3.5 It is inherent in any average, however, that it embraces figures greater and smaller than that amount. Therefore, whatever the overall average of land under trees may prove to be in Scotland by the time the pace of new planting is significantly less than it is now, some parts of the country will have a much higher density under trees than the overall average. Already, for example, we know from the Forestry Commission's 1980 census that, at that time, the average for Dumfries and Galloway Region was 21%. Grampian and Strathclyde Regions were next highest with around 15% and Central Region was close to the present overall Scottish average. Highland Region, however, was still well below average at about 9% which is perhaps more related to its extensive areas unsuitable for production timber, than a failure — relative to other regions — to take up this potential land use.

3.6   For our interests, however, it is the possible new areas which may develop much higher proportions of land under trees than the overall Scottish average, which especially demand attention. These areas may become more densely forested for several reasons. Extensive planting may occur in areas now having few forests. This is currently what is happening in parts of Caithness and more large scale planting may occur elsewhere in Scotland where little has been done so far. Or areas where there is now a scatter of small scale planting may be infilled by further planting to make larger blocks, perhaps as a consequence of marginal land going out of agriculture. Or open areas within existing extensively forested areas may be planted, thus creating even larger areas under trees, perhaps for example in the Southern Uplands or the eastern Highlands.

3.7   We are not alone in speculating on the reasons why such changes may come about. In the past, the simple fact of land suitable for planting becoming available for forestry has seldom been the only reason. Other, more or less important reasons according to circumstances, have been government policies for or against release of land from agriculture to forestry, land purchase costs, level of grant, fiscal arrangements, and various constraining factors such as water catchment or certain types of statutory designation (eg Sites of Special Scientific Interest). In the short term future — as earlier mentioned — land coming out of agriculture is currently foreseen as a major reason for more land going to forestry.

3.8   So, despite the difficulties and even feasibility of so doing in the opinion of some bodies, one of our policy conclusions deriving from the foregoing concern about new areas of extensive planting is that joint discussions should take place as to the desirable types and locations of major new planting. In Scotland, we see planning authorities, both regional and district where appropriate, as being key participants in such discussions which we believe could provide constructive opportunities for the formulation of indicative strategies for additional new planting in their areas. How much these indicative strategies would actually reduce conflicts of interest must be uncertain, but not to make the attempt and simply to continue to permit sectional interests and market forces to dictate how land is used, would seem to us to be a failure in collective responsibility.

5. Diverse landscapes are prized elements of our scenic heritage.

4 THE IMPACT OF FORESTRY ON LANDSCAPE

6. *Extensive afforestation, Borders.*

4.1   In the Foreword to our report *Scotland's Scenic Heritage,* published in 1978, it is stated that 'Scenic quality is essentially an aesthetic matter which does not readily lend itself to objective assessments' and in Part I of that report there is the further statement: 'We have not found or been able to develop any completely objective system capable of satisfactorily comprehending the selection of scenery in a way which would satisfy the essentially aesthetic aspects of the appreciation of natural beauty and amenity.' In short, although some perceptions are commonly agreed, what people like or dislike about the landscape of Scotland is largely a matter of personal preference.

4.2   This generalisation also applies to forests. Some people perceive forests as attractive elements in the landscape and some do not. Between these two perceptions there is every degree of variation, depending on many factors such as the kinds and mixtures of types of tree, whether forests are viewed from within or seen close to or from a distance, and their overall shape and pattern. Individual preferences are also influenced by special interests: such as in wildlife, hill walking, mountaineering or enjoyment of wilderness. Such special interests may be shared with the general interests of motorists driving through forested countryside, especially if planting has been carried out close to roads creating tunnel vision and obscuring views to loch or hill beyond.

4.3   Three general assertions can, however, be made with reasonable confidence. First, people do not like change in well-loved landscapes. Secondly, in time, people not only become used to changed landscapes, they may often find them attractive. Thirdly, variety is preferred to monotony. To quote again from *Scotland's Scenic Heritage,* 'richly diverse landscapes which combine prominent landforms, coastline, sea and fresh water lochs, rivers, woodlands and moorlands with some admixture of cultivated land are generally the most prized'. It is because of these preferences for variety that people so frequently voice their objections to post-war forest plantations which have often smoothed out the fine detail of land-form, obscured familiar views of sea, lochs and rivers, and converted former mixtures of small woods, moorland and inbye land into extensive areas of even-age monoculture planting, dissected by straight forest rides and with sharp edges, the whole superimposing geometric patterns on the natural sinuous flow of the countryside.

7. *Changed landscape can be attractive (Loch Tummel, Perthshire).*

4.4   We recognise, however, that many of these unwanted impacts of forestry on landscape are generally well understood within the industry, even if not always acted upon. As long ago as 1963, the Forestry Commission first employed Dame Sylvia Crowe as a consultant to advise on forest design and the Forestry Commission now employs three landscape architects and has plans to increase this number further, as well as running courses on forest design and management aimed at enhancing landscape and wildlife diversity. The major private forestry companies are now following this lead by employing their own environmental advisers and encouraging clients to be concerned about the appearance of forests. The recent publication of a code of practice by Timber Growers United Kingdom is further evidence of this wholly praiseworthy trend, although much will depend upon the extent to which practice on the ground always reflects these positive developments.

8. *Increasingly, attention will focus on the effects of forest management.*

4.5   The effect of this major effort by the industry to put its own house in order is that today new forests are usually designed and planted with significantly greater attention to landscape considerations than heretofore, but it has to be recognised by investors and advisers alike that extra costs or profits foregone may be involved in satisfying the needs of landscape and wildlife conservation. Unfortunately, although the fact that the past mistakes of foresters last a long time is an accepted truism, this does not lessen the continued visual impact of these mistakes. Therefore, notwithstanding that there will be opportunity to repair past mistakes by more sensitively designed second rotation forests and new forests, and notwithstanding the unplanned, sometimes beneficial effects of wind-throw on breaking up earlier geometric patterns, or a more welcoming attitude to self-sown species as positive enhancers of variety, concern about the appearance of forests continues to be widely expressed.

4.6   We consider that there is substance in this concern. The demands of clients and their financial advisers to make rapid progress in afforestation — for example to meet an April fiscal deadline — may continue on occasion to overrule how things ought to be done. There must also be concern for the future when, increasingly, attention will focus on the visual effects of forest management, rather than on afforestation. For example, the size and disposition of felling coupes, already a subject for occasional criticism, will attract greater attention as more forests reach the felling stage and, within mature forests, people who have come to enjoy walking through them will dislike scenes of temporary destruction. Therefore vigilance and care is imperative, not only in relation to new planting but also all aspects of ongoing forest management.

4.7   The continuing beauty of a forest depends on its health and ecological stability and it is therefore important that, as advocated in the World Conservation Strategy, the principle of sustainable utilisation of all the resources provided by a forest should be uppermost in the minds of forest planners and managers, and that practices which do least harm to soil and river systems are adopted as a matter of course.

9. *Good forestry enhances landscape character.*

4.8   The art and practice of forest design are now well developed. Forest plans should take full account of this knowledge and should articulate how the forest is to be planted and managed with a view to enhancing landscape character by:
— taking account of natural landforms;
— sensitive choice of species in some areas of the forest;
— avoiding hard edges to plantations by planting a variety of trees at wider spacing and in groups on forest boundaries;
— reinforcing existing broadleaved areas and planting new ones;
— ensuring that ploughing and conifer planting stops well short of water courses and water bodies;
— leaving some areas free of trees to maintain views from roads or footpaths;
— fostering the diversification of stand structure and species insofar as this is compatible with the broad aims of forest management;
— promoting diversity generally in the interests of nature conservation and public enjoyment;
— developing diversity of age class in single tracts of countryside and between intervisible tracts;
— designing felling coupes to fit into the landscape through careful consideration of their scale, shape and sequence of use;
— careful positioning of forest roads; and
— avoiding where possible line thinning regimes where they may appear obvious from frequented viewpoints.

5 THE IMPACT OF FORESTRY ON OTHER LAND USES

10. *Access to open hill land above plantations should be safeguarded.*

11. *Foresters should promote permissive access to forests.*

12. *Nature conservation objectives should be considered in siting and managing forests.*

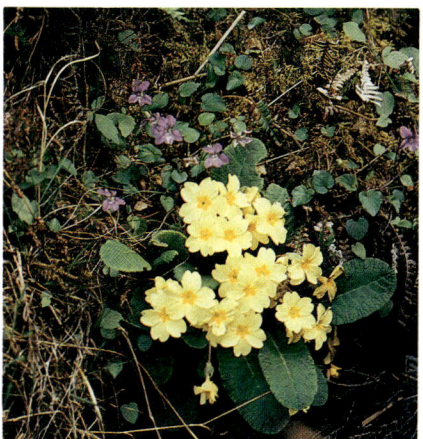

5.1   In this section, the impact of forestry on other land uses is reviewed. The review is incomplete and touches only lightly on some issues. For example, we have not commented on the effect of forestry on water catchment or on hydro-electricity generation, although we recognise that this can be important in some locations. Nevertheless, it is hoped that most of the main impacts currently the subject of debate have been identified.

5.2   **Recreation:** Several references have already been made to the recreational value of forests, in the context of their visual appearance. We recognise that, for outdoor recreation generally, a forest environment may be as attractive as one that is unwooded. What matters is the specific form of recreational activity and often, during the early planting stages, what people have been accustomed to prior to planting and before the forest has reached a more environmentally pleasing stage of maturity. Quite often, especially in hill country, there is a problem about maintaining access through new forests to unplanted land beyond. Much discontent about afforestation (as mentioned in 2.2) is because of its short or long-term damaging effect on recreational enjoyment of the countryside for rambling and hill walking. This is an issue which continuously needs to be kept to the forefront at the planning stage of new planting schemes and, wherever they occur, rights of way must be safeguarded. Where there are no public rights of way foresters should be prepared to take a much more positive attitude to permissive access to and through forests, particularly to facilitate access to high ground.

5.3   **Nature Conservation:** Although nature conservation can be a primary form of land use, for example in nature reserves, it is generally complementary to some other land use such as agriculture or forestry. In the context of our enabling legislation (the Countryside (Scotland) Act, 1967), the conservation of natural beauty includes the conservation of features of geological or physiographical interest and flora and fauna. From this it follows that, in general terms, many of our concerns and recommendations about forestry set out in this paper, embrace a concern for nature conservation.

5.4   However, because primary responsibility for nature conservation rests with other bodies, principally the Nature Conservancy Council, we recognise the importance of statements issued by such other bodies, notably in recent months the Council's draft discussion paper on 'Afforestation and Nature Conservation in Great Britain', now published. We welcomed the concluding recommendations of the draft paper which were useful and should have met with wide support. We also welcome the timely opportunity, consequent upon publication of our respective policy papers, for promoting a discussion involving a range of organisations aimed at seeking common ground. In some circumstances this common ground will be achieved only by compromise and by careful weighing of all land use interests.

5.5   The importance of wildlife to science, to the use of leisure time, to physical and mental health and to the quality of life, demands that it is catered for generally in the management of land and not solely in nature reserves. It is largely because these wider nature conservation objectives — for example as set out in 'Nature Conservation in Great Britain' published by the Nature Conservancy Council — are insufficiently recognised that some parts of the debate about forestry have been so vocal. Of particular concern are key habitats, such as certain peatlands, mid-altitude moorlands, river systems and upland semi-natural woodlands. We recognise that in regard to some of these natural ecosystems, change caused by afforestation or insensitive management of existing woodland may result in irreversible loss and thus that a sharply defined public concern about the impact of forestry on conservation of nature can on occasion be well justified.

13. *Land coming out of agriculture is a major reason for more land going to forestry.*

5.6   **Agriculture:** Currently, although there are still many issues about the effect of forestry on agriculture which require to be resolved, it is the converse which is the main subject of debate: that of new opportunities for the expansion of forestry on land which may become no longer economically viable for agriculture. The Countryside Commission for Scotland seeks to encourage a mixture of forestry and agriculture because it considers that the maintenance of a broad mosaic of land use in scale with the landscape is important, not solely because this best serves its interests in the maintenance of a diverse and therefore more attractive countryside, but also because it considers that a mix of land uses helps to encourage varied employment and a population living in as well as working in the countryside. Without a healthy rural population, public enjoyment of the countryside would be greatly diminished.

5.7   **Integration of Agriculture and Forestry:** For a variety of reasons, therefore, a workable balance must be retained between agriculture and forestry. Landholdings or estates taken out of agricultural use for forestry can have deleterious repercussions on neighbouring farms. For example, agricultural holdings in the uplands often depend upon the interchange of labour for sheep gathering, dipping and clipping; and therefore, for the mutual benefit of both agriculture and forestry as well as enhancement of the upland scene, integration of new plantings in scale with the landscape will best be achieved within existing farm structures. Such mixed land uses may result in different proportions of land going to forestry or to agriculture in different areas. We recognise that, at the level of the individual farm unit, the forestry to agriculture ratio may vary and yet each be equally appropriate, according to local circumstances, in terms of social balance, good agricultural practice and forestry.

5.8   However, an acceptable local balance of farming and forestry — be this termed integration or defined in some other way — has not yet been sufficiently eagerly sought by the collective efforts of central government departments, the forestry industry and other agencies. Existing consultation procedures could be used more imaginatively to foster the development of mixed enterprise units and there is a need for the concept of diversification and a mosaic of landscape uses to be developed more vigorously. The agricultural colleges could play a more entrepreneurial role in this regard, not only so as to help promote the concept but also in order to provide the specialist advice that will be required to run such mixed agriculture and forestry units efficiently. It should also be of help that the Department of Agriculture and Fisheries for Scotland are to acknowledge a presumption in favour of release of land to forestry in the case of upland and arable land — other than prime land — where the land forms part of a farm-forestry proposal promoted by a farmer.

5.9   We recognise that another possible consequence of revision of the agricultural support system may be an extension of forestry 'downhill' into lowland countryside. The release of better quality land for forestry may have various merits and demerits. For example, whereas enhanced opportunities may thereby occur for planting broadleaved trees on some better soils in a few parts of the country, a type of unco-ordinated coalescing of small blocks of conifer woodland into larger areas under trees may occur elsewhere without adequate overall regard to the scenic attractiveness of lowland countryside.

5.10   On balance, however, increased planting on lower ground should have desirable consequences if this is carried out with careful regard to landscape. It might reduce pressure on the higher land beloved by those seeking a 'wilderness experience'. It could reduce conflict between forestry and nature conservation since the new forests might be replacing improved grazings or even poor arable land rather than semi-natural vegetation of more nature conservation value. It would allow a wider range of species to be planted creating more varied and more valuable forests. Forests on better soils should be more wind-firm and more productive and because the land thus brought into forestry is likely to be that on which agriculture has been marginal, planting could enhance run down agricultural landscapes.

5.11   Increased planting in the countryside around towns would share these benefits with the added advantage that such woodlands can provide a beneficial potential for recreation near to where people live. We recognise that planting in urban fringe landscapes can present special problems. Nevertheless, the need for their enhancement in Scotland makes the establishment of such woodland highly desirable. Our experience in helping to establish the Central Scotland Countryside Trust has convinced us of the considerable scope for tree planting in the countryside around towns, and that this is an activity in which collaboration by many bodies is a key to success.

5.12 Field Sports: Field sports, such as fishing, pheasant and grouse shooting, and deer stalking, are other land uses on which forestry can have major impacts, with consequential 'knock-on' effects on the changing appearance of the countryside and its enjoyment. There is a long standing relationship between lowland broadleaved woodland and the attractions of pheasant shooting which can be of positive benefit for the creation and maintenance of small scale mixed plantings in the fabric of the countryside. This relationship should have a bearing on the purposes for which grant for small plantings is given, which should not be overlooked by bodies giving grant for tree planting mainly for such other purposes as amenity, shelter and wood production. The relationship between forests, acid deposition and fish stocks in parts of Scotland is currently the subject of research and debate and we believe that the appropriate authorities should respond to widespread public concern about this issue.

5.13 Grouse Moors: In landscape terms, the purple colouring of heather moorland is a highly attractive by-product of grouse moor management. However, the economics and the status of grouse will determine whether this form of land use is maintained at the present extent or will give way to more intensive agriculture or to forestry. In the past, the main loss has been to sheep walk, particularly in the Southern Uplands and this, of course, has maintained the open, unwooded character of the hills. Latterly, and particularly in the Eastern Grampians, land use change from grouse moorland has largely been to forestry. We recognise that people hold different opinions on the extent to which forestry and grouse moors make good neighbours. Burning, in the interests of good heather management, can place forests at risk and forests may increase predation by foxes on neighbouring grouse moors and upland farms.

5.14 Red Deer: The issues in relation to forestry and red deer are rather different. Deer can inflict serious and even catastrophic damage in both planted areas and natural woodlands. The size, location and design of plantations is of vital importance for protection, while fencing for forestry can significantly reduce land previously available for winter grazing and can also impede the traditional movement of deer onto and off higher ground. Co-ordination of objectives is essential when afforestation takes place over ground previously occupied by red deer and in some situations a policy of heavy culling may be required in order to reduce movement of deer forced out of their previous grazings onto agricultural ground. Nevertheless, care will be required in any change of deer management where deer stalking is an important land use on neighbouring land and both afforestation and culling should of course be done in consultation with the Red Deer Commission and neighbouring deer forest owners.

5.15 We recognise that the subject of deer and forestry raises substantial matters of detail which require resolution, for example in regard to the possible need for additional deer-fencing grant where integration of forestry and agriculture is to be encouraged. This may be desirable not only for exclusion of red deer but also other species of deer. In this, however, as for many other land uses, it is not appropriate in this policy paper to set out at length every matter in contention. We simply acknowledge that deer of all species have no regard for the boundaries of land ownership and therefore, due consideration must be given to the significance of their economics wherever they impinge on the rural life of Scotland.

5.16 Archaeology: Scotland has a rich archaeological heritage which is of considerable cultural, historical and educational importance. Archaeological sites arouse interest in the landscape by indicating the passage of time and marking the effects of man on the land in past ages. Landowners have a statutory obligation under the Ancient Monuments Act, 1979, to protect any scheduled ancient monument, field monuments or historic buildings on their property. Scheduled features, however, represent only a small proportion of known sites and the value of some other sites can only be guessed at in the absence of formal surveys or excavation. Afforestation procedures should not only seek to avoid damaging archaeological features but provision should also be made to allow access to sites for educational, scientific or recreational purposes. The 'Forestry and Woodland Code' published by Timber Growers United Kingdom recommends the need for consultation with trained archaeologists before afforestation proceeds. This is a matter to which the planning authority should ensure sufficient attention is given during the consultation process referred to in paragraph 9.5.

14. *Reconstructed clachan, Tummel Forest.*

15. *Red deer stag.*

6 BROADLEAVES

6.1   In terms of scenic resources, the importance of broadleaved woods and trees and the special problems involved in maintaining or enhancing this resource, especially in Scotland, are well known. Because broadleaved woods are an integral part of some of the most widely appreciated landscapes and in many areas their importance greatly exceeds their size, broadleaved woods should be promoted in areas where such woodland cover is sparse. Broadleaved trees should be given a positive role in coniferous forests, particularly where they offer the greatest environmental benefit and can enhance the appearance of plantations, for example in the second rotation when site conditions may have been ameliorated.

6.2   For these reasons, as well as the benefits which broadleaved woodlands can provide for the recreational enjoyment of countryside and for wildlife, we welcome the recent government statement on broadleaves and will be seeking to play a positive role with the Forestry Commission and other bodies in helping to implement the new broadleaves policy. We concur with the Forestry Commission that only in exceptional cases should areas of broadleaved woodland be converted to some other purpose and that a sustained and co-ordinated effort will be required to promote and provide for new broadleaved planting. The necessity for retaining and reinforcing all broadleaved woods which fall within areas to be afforested should also be emphasised. We consider that broadleaved woods should be encouraged in all appropriate places where they reinforce their important role in the scenic fabric of the countryside and that continuing effort should be made to bring all broadleaved woodland into management under the principles set out in the Forestry Commission's 'Guidelines for the Management of Broadleaved Woodland'.

6.3   We shall continue to welcome applications for grant for broadleaved planting of areas less than 0.25 hectares in the countryside, under our grant scheme for amenity planting, notwithstanding that the cost of such schemes will be significantly higher per unit area than larger planting proposals. Native species have a crucial role in supporting a wide range of wildlife and in creating landscapes of local character. Under our grant scheme, therefore, we shall continue to promote the planting of native species, but not exclusively so. For example, in gardens and designed landscapes we shall continue to enable the planting of a much wider range of species in order to maintain and enhance their interest and to give grant on species which have been traditionally planted in Scotland and have become accepted and admired elements in our countryside.

16. Oakwood, Cuilvona, Stirlingshire.

7 CALEDONIAN PINE

17. *Broadleaved woods are an integral part of widely appreciated landscape.*

18. *Scots pine, Torridon, Ross and Cromarty.*

7.1   The native Scots pine forms distinctive woodlands in the Scottish landscape. These remnants of the once much more extensive Caledonian pine forest are greatly valued for the wealth of their wildlife, their beauty, and their unique Scottish quality. The need to conserve these woods is now widely recognised and detailed management regimes are practised in certain forests. However, there is still a need to ensure that all remnants of Calendonian pine forests are carefully managed with due regard given to their scenic and scientific importance and for the pleasure that they can give to people walking within them.

7.2   Although the Native Pinewood Grant Scheme administered by the Forestry Commission goes some way towards providing for their expansion and sustained management, less than half of the remnants under private ownership have as yet been brought under this scheme. Consideration should therefore be given to bringing the level of grant available under that scheme at least up to that which is available under the Broadleaved Woodland Grant Scheme, and further effort given to encouraging owners to safeguard this exceptionally important type of woodland. Guidelines for the management of native pinewoods, analogous to those available for broadleaved woodland should be developed and adherence to these guidelines should be a condition of the availability of grant. Also, because native Scots pinewoods are such valuable and characteristic features of the Scottish landscape but exist in limited remnants, we consider that our proposal for a higher rate of grant for the Native Pinewood Grant Scheme should be extended to the planting of new native pinewoods and to fostering natural regeneration on currently unforested sites in areas where seed of local provenance can be used. The management of these new woods should also follow the proposed guidelines. The Forestry Commission should therefore give consideration to extending the areas within which Native Pinewood Grant is available.

19. *Caledonian pine forest is greatly valued for its beauty and unique Scottish quality.*

8 FORESTRY ECONOMICS AND GRANTS

8.1   Debate about the economic rationale for afforestation ranges between those who, basing forecasts on future supply, demand and prices, conclude that there is a need for increased rates of afforestation, and those who, using different forecasts and invoking the principle of comparative trading advantage, conclude that there is no justification for further planting and that much recent afforestation is economically unsound. We believe that the quality of long-term economic forecasting is such that there is room for doubt about attaching too much weight to the conclusions to be drawn from either side. However, the less readily quantified benefits accruing from landscape and wildlife conservation, amenity, informal recreation and other social purposes, such as rural employment, must also be included in any appraisal of forestry proposals. We believe that, after giving due weight to these factors, there is a good case for more forestry in Scotland. It is important, therefore, that these broader benefits be considered in plans for afforestation and management of all forests, and for every effort to be made to maximise the benefits from the multiple use of forest areas.

8.2   **Fiscal Support:** However, the fiscal support structure for forestry does not necessarily encourage such policies. Support through tax relief gives the greatest benefit to the most profitable forms of forestry leaving marginally economic or uneconomic woodland management relatively poorly supported. Nevertheless, the current tax and grant system does not act particularly against, for instance, the management of broadleaved woodlands; rather, our concern is that the level of support is inadequate to redress the underlying poor economic performance of much woodland of importance for its contribution to scenery and nature conservation. Contrariwise, it is probable that change to the fiscal arrangements would have considerable unfavourable impact on land management in general because of the inter-relations between land values and fiscal structures, and that providing equivalent support through a system of grants would demand exceedingly high planting grants or possibly costly annual management grants. The Commission recognises that the current system brings considerable amounts of money into the rural estate which might otherwise be invested elsehere and would not necessarily be captured by the Treasury for reinvestment in forestry through a different system. That said, what is important is that both grant and tax foregone should provide the best possible range of social benefit.

8.3   In the last eleven years we have found the selective incentive of conditional exemption from Capital Transfer Tax, of land of value to the national heritage, a useful encouragement to sensitive countryside management. Under the newly proposed Inheritance Tax these opportunities will continue largely unchanged and we consider that an extension of the principle of conditional rather than automatic relief should apply to other fiscal arrangements in such a way as to be equally beneficial to ensuring sensitive forest management. In a later section (paragraphs 9.3 to 9.7) we propose the idea of a planting licence administered by the Forestry Commission. This, in effect, would make assessment to tax of commercial forestry under Schedule D conditional upon approval by the Forestry Commission that the proposed forest was socially and environmentally welcome. The availability of Schedule B on change of ownership is a special and major concession to commercial forestry, and we argue that this too should be available only on condition of Forestry Commission approval of a plan of operations that — as part of the plan for productive timber — demonstrates the intention to manage the woods in a way which is compatible with the broad aims of overall forest policy for landscape and wildlife conservation, recreation and social benefits. Consideration could be given to allowing a change from Schedule D to B to take place without the prior need for a change of ownership for woodlands managed on very long rotations.

20. *Scots pine forms distinctive and characteristic woodlands in the Scottish landscape.*

8.4   Making tax relief conditional in this way raises the question as to whether the decisions made by the Forestry Commission should be open to appeal. We recognise that this is an important issue for consideration but suggest that the balanced forum provided by an expanded Regional Advisory Committee (paragraph 9.9) might help in the conciliatory resolution of such cases, while leaving an opportunity for a final reference to Ministers.

8.5   In concluding this section on fiscal support, we observe that over the next 20 years or so the forest industry will be moving from a situation in which the main aim has been to create a resource to one in which that resource is managed in accordance with principles of sustainable ultilisation. The present fiscal system has effectively supported the current phase but it may be that a different structure will be more appropriate to the sort of forestry which society will require in the 21st century. This will need careful thought and consideration over the coming years.

8.6   **Grant:** We recognise the importance of keeping under close review levels of grant for planting, from whatever source. Opinions on whether current levels of grant are sufficient inducement much depend on whether or not such grant is associated with an ability to secure tax benefits against other income, on the costs of land acquisition, the size of area to be planted and other factors. In the context of integration of farming and forestry discussed earlier (5.5) there are a number of issues to be considered. Fiscal benefits for farmers depend upon their having sufficient taxable income to enable them to benefit from this support, whilst tenant farmers may be unable to participate because of constraints in land tenure legislation and possible a reluctance to become committed to a crop with such a long rotation as forestry.

8.7   **Article 20:** There is also an important issue concerning Article 20 of the European Economic Community Council Regulation No 797/85 (Agricultural Structures Directive), whereby member states may give grants to agricultural holdings for the afforestation of agricultural land and for investment in woodland improvements involving the provision of shelterbelts, firebreaks and water points and for forest roads. We are aware that the British Government has not given effect to Article 20 and several respondents to our discussion paper, in which we recommended the use of Article 20, expressed doubt as to why Government should do so. Even so, Article 20 does appear to provide an improved opportunity for integration of forestry and agriculture and we consider that this issue should be re-examined by Government or some new measures introduced specifically appropriate to Britain. We take this view because of the potential advantages which Article 20 appears to provide for opening up a support system for woodland planting on farms, of a type to which farmers are already accustomed, and because the level of assistance thereby provided could help to offset the fact that many low-income farmers are unable to obtain the tax benefits currently available for forestry.

8.8   **The Integrated Farm Forestry Investment Scheme:** As another means whereby to help farmers bridge the gap between planting and a first cash return, we recognise the potential beneficial role of an Integrated Farm Forestry Investment scheme recently proposed by the Highlands and Islands Development Board (see Annex 2).

9 CONTROLS

9.1   Coincident with two recent cases involving planting without grant approval from the Forestry Commission, and a growing concern over the damage caused to the physical environment by certain afforestation practices, public support for the imposition of planning controls over afforestation has increasingly been widely canvassed. The Countryside Commission for Scotland does not favour the extension of statutory planning control to include afforestation. It is not persuaded that such control would be any more conducive to securing good decisions about the management of land or be as adaptable or efficient, as an improved consultation system applied with the necessary rigour by the Forestry Commission exercising its newly expressed forestry responsibilities for the conservation of the countryside.

9.2   It is therefore towards the strengthening of the existing system to achieve its effective implementation that our recommendatitions are directed. It has already been agreed that we should be consulted on afforestation schemes over 50 hectares in extent in the 40 National Scenic Areas designated in Scotland and both in NSAs and elsewhere in Scotland we are increasingly being afforded the opportunity to comment constructively on applications for forestry grant schemes. However, there is room for improvement to ensure that the consultation process works to best effect and that afforestation is in fact carried out with great sensitivity. If such efforts are unsuccessful, then the current rumblings of discontent are likely to grow louder, along with more clamant demands for the extension of statutory planning controls to include afforestation.

9.3   **A Planting Licence:**   One alternative to planning control which could be developed would be a form of planting licence administered by the Forestry Commission, analogous to the existing system of felling licences. This could avoid the need for amending the fiscal system in such a way as to prevent tax relief on planting without grant approval. There would need to be a minimum area below which a planting licence would not be required and we propose an area of about 5 to 10 hectares as appropriate for most situations in terms of landscape conservation, while still allowing small plantings for shelter and amenity to proceed without licence. Planting adjacent to existing woodland which would result in the creation of a discrete forest area greater than the minimum agreed area would similarly require a licence. Legislation affecting the whole of Britain would, of course, be required before a licence system could be implemented in Scotland and we recognise that in its detailed provisions, lower or higher minimum areas might be suggested for other parts of the country and should be given careful consideration.

9.4   Before issuing a licence for planting in excess of whatever minimal area is agreed, it should be a requirement that the Forestry Commission consults with the appropriate planning authority. Although the actual decisions should be left to the Forestry Commission, we recognise that public acceptance of the benefits of a planting licence would be greatly diminished or even, in some quarters, considered a disbenefit, in the absence of effective consultation arrangements and, where necessary, advice from Regional Advisory Committees. Thus some prior consultation should take place but we consider that it would be inappropriate to expect the Forestry Commission to have to make a judgement as to which bodies should be consulted amongst the many that might wish to offer views, except where there is some existing arrangement for special categories of land.

9.5   We consider that the Forestry Commission should look to the planning authorities as being best placed to carry out this wider consultation and we therefore recommend that the Forestry Commission should so refine the existing consultation system that there is automatic consultation with the appropriate planning authorities for all afforestation schemes greater than the agreed minimal area. The planning authority should ensure that all interests are considered through a process of appropriately wide consultation, where necessary both amongst statutory and voluntary bodies. While recognising that for a few authorities in Scotland this may produce a slightly greater involvement than has been the case, our basic premise is that increasingly planning authorities must be seen to contribute to decisions on rural land use and thus be consulted. Furthermore, a more generally applied system of consultation with planning authorities should encourage the preparation of indicative strategies for forestry, taking account of other rural land uses, which should assist in reducing the time taken to respond to individual cases.

9.6   It is unnecessary that this consultation should place an additional rung on the existing ladder of consultation. Proposals for a licence should be accompanied by a comprehensive plan for the proposed forest area and consultation would take place on it prior to issuing the licence. The plan would need to state precisely how account is taken of landscape and nature conservation, recreation, and other conservation interests. Payment of grant would follow granting of a planting licence. In areas less than the agreed minimum, applications for grants and existing consultation arrangements (which in Scotland vary between authorities) could proceed as at present. In future, however, other forms of consultation with statutory agencies relating to areas of particular interest for the conservation of the scenic or scientific interest may need to be strengthened.

9.7   In practice, we recognise that the need to issue a separate planting licence might not be necessary for schemes also receiving grant from the Forestry Commission In a similar way to the regulations controlling the felling of trees, operations in accordance with an approved plan of operations under one of the Forestry Commission's grant schemes would not require a licence. Agreement to pay grant could be deemed to embrace also the planting licence. In that case, however, the observations made in 9.3.2-4 about the need for consultation before issuing a planting licence would need to be extended to approval of planting grant. At this stage we do not have a view as to which arrangement would provide the most effective safeguard for our interests and await consideration of whatever detailed scheme in due course is proposed.

9.8   **Conservation Plans:** In our discussion paper we referred to the need for forest conservation plans, in this case, intending conservation to embrace all countryside subjects which may require to be conserved. In responses to that paper, some forestry bodies expressed concern about what was thought to be implied: that a separate document covering conservation issues over and above the plan of operations should be prepared. However, other bodies representing conservation interests welcomed the idea. So as to be quite clear on this matter, our concern is not whether there is a separate piece of paper setting out how conservation interests are to be accommodated but that in deciding what land is afforested and in planning the design and management of a forest, explicit account is taken of conservation requirements. If in certain circumstances, forest managers see it as helpful to prepare separate conservation plans, then this will be welcomed but we do not consider that such plans should necessarily in every case be required before approval of a Forestry Grant Scheme. What is important is that all forestry plans should not only include clear and adequate resolution of all conservation and recreation needs, but that readers of the plan should be able readily to identify wherein these issues are dealt with, perhaps by referring to each under separate headings: such as landscape, wildlife, amenity, recreation or archaeology.

9.9   **Regional Advisory Committees:** The Regional Advisory Committees (RACs) have a crucial role in seeking to resolve disagreement over afforestation proposals which have aroused conflict. Although such conflicts are rare, it is necessary that extreme care is taken in coming to a decision over the future use of an area of land where opinions and interests may differ markedly. Because of this critical position, it is widely felt that the role of the RACs is in need of revision and that the required legislation should be promoted. We therefore welcome the recommendations of a recent consultation paper issued by the Forestry Commission which allows for the representation of a broader range of interests on the RACs than at present, thus reflecting a more publicly acceptable balance between forestry and other interests. In the course of giving effect to this measure, we agree also that RACs should be chaired by people known to have a balanced appreciation of all major land use interests — as earlier recommended in our discussion paper — and that the new procedures should permit a range of views to be placed before the committees, who should thereafter inform people submitting views of the outcome, thereby enabling the proceedings of RACs to be made more public.

10 TRAINING

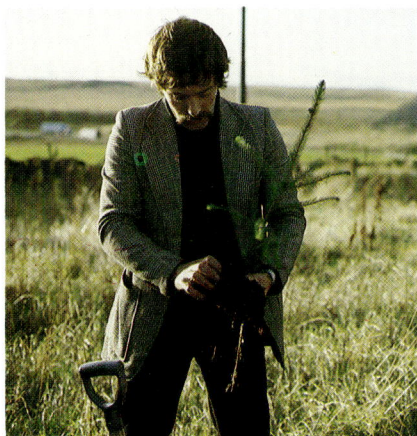

21. Instruction in tree planting.

10.1   One of the most frequently identified consequences of the current debate about land use, particularly in the context of integration of farming and forestry, has been the need for retraining of people managing land in ways traditional to their own specialist expertise, so as to encourage diversification into other forms of land use. We support this conclusion. Because of our experience in giving grant for amenity planting, we are especially aware of the widespread lack of skills in the planting and management of small woods for a variety of purposes and the effective use of small-wood forest products for a range of rural uses.

10.2   Thus we consider that there is a need for training — particularly amongst the farming community — to develop skills in tree planting and management of small woods. Concerted collective action is required and closer integration of training opportunities amongst the Agricultural Colleges, Agricultural Training Board, Forestry Training Council, Universities and other appropriate training bodies. These training needs, however, extend beyond the planting and management of trees and woods for wood production, to training for the integrated management of land generally for scenic and wildlife conservation, recreation and other special interests. We look forward to contributing in as positive a way as our resources allow, both to participating in and to helping enable others to improve training for future land use needs in Scotland.

22. Training for the integrated management of land is becoming necessary for Scotland's diverse landscape.

11 RESEARCH

23. Planting on lower ground can have desirable consequences when done with regard to the landscape.

11.1   We recognise the important role of the Forestry Commission's Forestry Research Co-ordination Committee in keeping under review the whole subject area of forest research, and that there are many aspects of such research — for example in relation to timber quality, harvesting and so on — that are only distantly relevant to our own interests. Nevertheless, increasingly there are aspects of forest research which relate to environmental considerations in regard to which we have a direct interest and we therefore look forward in future to working more closely with the Forestry Research Co-ordination Committee than is provided for at present simply by having the opportunity to comment on the work of individual review groups set up by the Committee.

24. Research into the impact of forestry practice on the environment should lead to improved practices with benefits in landscape appearance, amenity and recreation experience.
(a) and (b) Ploughing and ditching.
(c) Deer in forest.
(d) Harvesting.

12 PRIVATISATION

12.1   The Countryside Commission for Scotland does not welcome some recent speculation about privatisation of the Forestry Commission and it considers that concerted vigilance is required against the possibility of this idea being further promoted. We regard the present mixed economy in the composition of the forestry industry as essentially beneficial to rural areas and that divorcing the Forestry Authority function from that of Forestry Enterprise would be greatly to the detriment of the former activity.

12.2   The Forestry Commission has played and must continue to play a key role in the assimilation of forestry into the Scottish countryside. As Forestry Authority, it is essential to the proper administration of controls over felling and planting through licences and grants, in encouraging and influencing the private sector in positive ways as evidenced by its research and development work, its advisory publications and its assistance in safety and training, and in ensuring the rational development of a timber resource capable of producing security of supply and quantity to downstream industry. Equally, its Forestry Enterprise greatly facilitates this role as Forestry Authority and is of value in itself as an example to the private sector and because the Forestry Commission's broader statutory requirements provide benefits in the countryside which may not always be taken into account by private forestry interests. National Forest Parks, Forestry Commission recreational facilities and its expertise in forest landscaping, all demonstrate this recognition of wider values which could helpfully be emulated by the private sector.

25. Pine logs stacked after felling.

13 REVIEW

13.1   Earlier, we have commented on the considerable number of conferences and reports on forestry, listed in Appendix 2. All this activity will be of little long-term value if it does not lead to improvements on the ground, in the countryside. As well as giving increased attention to forestry under the specific headings identified earlier in this paper, there will be a need to take stock again in a more general way in about five years and in our forward planning that intention will be recorded.

14 CONCLUSIONS AND RECOMMENDATIONS

14.1   In this final section, the Countryside Commission for Scotland's general policy on forestry is summarised and specific initiatives recommended to enable these policy aims to be achieved. The policies are formulated in the context of our statutory interests as stated in 1.1.

14.2   The policies recognise that:

— most of the continued growth of forestry in Britain is going to take place in Scotland, and at a greater pace than elsewhere,
— this will predominantly be carried out by the private sector,
— afforestation will be the main cause for change in the appearance of the Scottish countryside,
— change is an inherent characteristic of the countryside.

14.3   The policies also accept the existence of a thriving forestry industry, both in the public and private sectors, aimed at maintaining and developing British forest products and their effective marketing, because of the benefits which forestry can bring to the rural life of Scotland, on which enjoyment of the countryside much depends. Because of its statutory responsibilities, the Countryside Commission for Scotland is well placed to make its views known and to advise government on developments which occur in the Scottish countryside, spanning the whole spectrum of rural land use, conservation and development policies.

POLICY

26. Sitka spruce.

14.4   We therefore state as our own policies that we shall be increasingly vigilant about, and will seek to influence:

— the location, extent and design of further afforestation,
— the relationship of forestry to other land uses,
— the manner in which afforestation is carried out, and
— the manner in which harvesting and restocking take place, in terms of the effects which forest management has on the appearance and enjoyment of the countryside.

14.5   We reaffirm our present policy that we do not support statutory planning control of afforestation. Meeting our concerns will require strengthening of the consultation system and commitment by all those involved to give full regard to all interests, while recognising the importance of production forestry.

INITIATIVES

14.6   **How Much More Afforestation?:** We view the next 20 years or so as the last in a period during which there is major afforestation of Scotland's countryside and speculate that thereafter a more stable form of rotational forestry will continue on a land area of around 17-20% of Scotland's land area (3.3). To help ensure that afforestation in this phase is integrated harmoniously into the countryside we consider that joint discussion should take place with other agencies and central and local government as to the desirable types and locations of major new planting and the likely impacts afforestation will have on other land uses and on the appearance of the Scottish countryside. Such discussions should assist planning authorities to prepare indicative strategies for forestry development in their areas which in turn will facilitate the consultation procedure and allow for improved forward planning of forestry developments (3.8).

14.7   **The Impact of Forestry on Landscape:** We recognise the advances made in forest design over the years (4.4). However, the industry must consistently give effect to the stated intention to ensure that all planting and forest management is carried out with careful regard for scenic and recreational interests. To this end, Forestry Grant Scheme approval should be given only where plans take explicit account of scenic, recreation, nature conservation and archaeological interests as set out in the 'Forestry and Woodland Code' published by Timber Growers United Kingdom and in the Forestry Commission's broadleaves policy. Similar forestry plans should be developed for existing forests to ensure that these interests are taken into full account during management operations and are strengthened in second generation forests. We therefore urge all landowners seeking to afforest land to ensure that plans going forward for approval are adequately detailed in the resolution of all interests, so as to ensure speedy progress through the consultation system (9.8).

14.8   The industry should determine to use 'best practices' during afforestation, forest management, harvesting and restocking with a view to minimising adverse hydrological and soil effects. The industry should reaffirm that the aim of all practices is to ensure sustainable utilisation of the forest, its soils and water for the range of benefits which forests can provide (4.7).

14.9   In regard to the scenic interest, special care should be taken in the planning of new forests and the harvesting and restocking of existing forests with a view to enhancing landscape character. This concern should be clearly articulated in plans seeking grant scheme approval and in plans of operations (4.8).

14.10   **Recreation:** Special consideration should be given to recreation in the planning of new forests, both so as to enhance opportunities for recreation within forest environments and to protect and promote access routes through the new forests from roadside public access points to unplanted land beyond. Any existing rights of way should be safeguarded. Permissive access should be promoted in and through existing forests (5.2).

14.11   **Nature Conservation:** We recognise that the conservation of the beauty of the countryside is closely related to the conservation of nature, and that part of the pleasure which people derive from visiting forests arises from the variety of wildlife and other natural features experienced (5.3). Therefore, we support the continued need for the forestry industry to plan for and promote practices which will enhance the nature conservation value of forests, not just in areas of particular interest but throughout the whole forest estate and to have regard for the nature conservation value of existing habitats when determining the siting and extent of new afforestation (5.5).

14.12   **Integration of Forestry and Agriculture:** Greater effort should be made to encourage a balanced mixture of agriculture and forestry so as to ensure a mosaic of land uses and a diversity of rural employment opportunities (5.6). Thus:

— there should be closer collaboration between the forestry industry, the Department of Agriculture and Fisheries for Scotland and the agricultural advisory services, aimed at giving effect to greater integration of agriculture and forestry (5.8);
— the implications for forestry moving 'downhill' as a possible consequence of the release of land from agriculture should be given more serious consideration by all bodies having an interest in this issue including ourselves, both in the context of diversifying the economics of existing farm units in preference to whole farms changing to forestry and with a view to opportunities for enhanced planting of broadleaved woodlands and more productive conifer plantations in the better soils and climates of low ground (5.10);
— the government should re-examine Article 20 of the European Economic Community Council Agricultural Structures Directive in more positive terms than heretofore, because of the opportunities which this Article provides for new forms of grant for integration of forestry and agriculture or some new national measure should be developed which is specifically appropriate to Britain (8.7).

14.13   **Field Sports:** As with agriculture, we recognise a need for careful consideration to be given to the integration of forestry with field sports and the management of red deer which often are important land uses on neighbouring land as well as being a potential valuable subsidiary land use in woodlands (5.12 to 5.15).

14.14 **Broadleaves:** We welcome the new broadleaves policy of the Forestry Commission and will seek to support it both through our advice and through our own grant scheme for amenity planting which is available for planting areas of trees less than 0.25 hectares in the countryside (6.2 and 6.3).

14.15 **Caledonian Pine:** Caledonian pine woodlands are a unique Scottish resource for wildlife and scenery. Their conservation is vital. This should be furthered by increasing the rate of grant available under the Native Pinewood Grant Scheme of the Forestry Commission and promoting the scheme to relevant landowners. Guidelines for the management of Caledonian pinewoods, analogous to those available for broadleaved wood, should be developed and adherence to such guidance should be a condition of the availability of grant. The Forestry Commission should consider extending their Native Pinewood Grant Scheme to the creation of new native pinewoods (7.2).

14.16 **Controls on Forestry:** Although we do not support the call for statutory planning control over new afforestation, we do see a need to devise a more effective system of controls and incentives:

— new planting should be subject to approval from the Forestry Commission, under a form of planting licence (9.3);
— before issuing a licence or approving applications under its grant schemes for proposals to afforest areas greater than some minimum area (we suggest in the region of 5-10 hectares), it should be a requirement for the Forestry Commission to consult the appropriate planning authority who in turn should consult appropriate statutory and voluntary bodies where necessary to ensure that all interests are taken into account in the siting, designing and proposed development of a new forest (9.4 and 9.5);
— to help in this process, local authorities should prepare indicative strategies for forestry in their area which can be used as a basis for response to consultation (3.8 and 9.5);
— to enable rapid decision making in this consultation process, it should be a requirement that all applicants seeking a licence or approval for grant should submit a comprehensive plan wherein the resolution of all conservation and development issues can be readily identified, perhaps by referring to each under separate headings (4.7, 4.8 and 9.8);
— in order to deal effectively with controversial applications, the Regional Advisory Committees of the Forestry Commission should have a broad and balanced membership under a non-partisan chairman. We therefore support the view that they should have an enlarged membership to allow for this and that their findings should be made public (9.9);
— as an incentive to sensitive forest siting, design and management, we consider that tax relief to commercial forestry under Schedules D and B should only be available as a consequence of Forestry Commission approval that a proposed plan of operation is in full accordance with conservation principles and national forestry policy. Effective administration of a licensing system would have this effect over election to Schedule D. We suggest that reversion of the assessment of commercial woodland to Schedule B should similarly only proceed given Forestry Commission assurance that these principles are being applied in management (8.3).

14.17 **Training:** A wider spectrum of people than at present — particularly amongst the farming community — should be encouraged to develop skills in tree planting and management of small woods. There should be closer integration in development of training opportunities amongst the Agricultural Colleges, the Forestry Training Council and other appropriate bodies (10.1).

14.18 We should jointly re-examine, with the aforementioned bodies, the Forestry Commission and the Nature Conservancy Council, opportunities for training in the integrated management of land, especially management for landscape and wildlife conservation, recreation provision and other special interests (10.2).

14.19 **Research:** Because increasingly there are aspects of forestry research which relate to our interests, we look forward to working more closely with the Forestry Research Co-ordination Committee (11.1).

14.20 **Privatisation of the Forestry Commission:** The Countryside Commission for Scotland is strongly against privatisation of the Forestry Commission, in whole or in part (12.1).

14.21 **Review:** We propose to review our policy in regard to forestry in about five years (13.1).

Appendix 1

**LIST OF BODIES WHO SUBMITTED COMMENTS ON:
'FORESTRY IN SCOTLAND' A DISCUSSION PAPER ISSUED BY
THE COUNTRYSIDE COMMISSION FOR SCOTLAND**

Association for the Protection of Rural Scotland
Badenoch and Strathspey Conservation Group
Botanical Society for the British Isles
Convention of Scottish Local Authorities
Council for British Archaeology Scotland
Countryside Commission (England and Wales)
Crofters Commission
Department of Agriculture and Fisheries for Scotland
Forestry Commission
Friends of the Earth (Scotland)
Highlands and Islands Development Board
Institute of Chartered Foresters
Ladies' Scottish Climbing Club
Landscape Institute
Mountaineering Council of Scotland
National Farmers' Union of Scotland
National Trust for Scotland
Nature Conservancy Council
North East Mountain Trust
Ramblers' Association (Scottish Council)
Red Deer Commission
Royal Institution of Chartered Surveyors (Scottish Branch)
Royal Scottish Forestry Society
Royal Society for Nature Conservation
Royal Society for the Protection of Birds
Royal Town Planning Institute (Scottish Branch)
Rural Forum
Saltire Society
Scottish Civic Trust
Scottish Countryside Activities Council
Scottish Countryside Rangers Association
Scottish Development Department
Scottish Landowners' Federation
Scottish Rights of Way Society Ltd
Scottish Scenic Trust
Scottish Wild Land Group
Scottish Wildlife Trust
Timber Growers United Kingdom
Vincent Wildlife Trust
Woodland Trust
World Wildlife Fund UK

27. Douglas fir.

Appendix 2

ANNOTATED LIST OF SELECTED PUBLICATIONS (1982-1986) AND OF RECENT SEMINARS AND CONFERENCES RELATING TO FORESTRY IN SCOTLAND

1 Forest Policy

In 1984-85, the Forestry Commission produced two consultative documents leading up to their Broadleaves Policy announced in September 1985 and described in detail in three publications produced in October of that year. Others have also been looking at current forest policy. The European Commission produced a paper on community action in the forestry sector in 1986, and in specific regard to Scotland, the Friends of the Earth (Scotland) published their suggestions for a green forestry policy late in 1984. Following the Wildlife and Countryside (Amendment) Act 1985 laying upon the Forestry Commission a requirement to seek a balance between timber production and wildlife conservation, in 1986 it published a revised statement of its policy in regard to nature conservation and at about the same time issued a discussion paper on proposed changes to be made to the composition and working of its Regional Advisory Committees.

FOE (Scotland) (1984): *A Forest Policy for Scotland*
Forestry Commission (1984): *Broadleaves in Britain: A Consultative Paper*
Forestry Commission (1985): *Broadleaves in Britain: Review of Policy*
Forestry Commission (1985): *The Policy for Broadleaved Woodland*
Forestry Commission (1985): *Broadleaved Woodland Grant Scheme*
Forestry Commission (1985): *Guidelines for the Management of Broadleaved Woodland*
European Commission (1986): *Discussion Paper on Community Action in the Forestry Sector*
Forestry Commission (1986): *The Forestry Commission and Conservation; Policy and Procedure Paper No 4*
Forestry Commission (1986): *The Composition and Procedures of the Forestry Commission's Regional Advisory Committees: A Consultation Paper*

2 Forestry and Agriculture

The agriculture departments, together with the Forestry Commission, addressed themselves to reviewing the potential for woodland as a farm crop to help ease possible constraints on the agricultural industry imposed by review of the common agricultural policy. Earlier, James Hunter had analysed the future of hill and upland farming for Rural Forum with some regard being paid to more forestry taking place in farm units. The Scottish Branch of the Royal Institution of Chartered Surveyors looked closely at this topic too, and later, the Highlands and Islands Development Board announced a scheme which may bring investors and farmers together under limited partnership to create areas of forestry on farms. Speculation on possible changes in agricultural structures prompted the Nature Conservancy Council to contract consultants to examine what changes are likely to occur in land use in the years up to the end of the century. In response to a Parliamentary Question, on 24 March 1986 the Secretary of State for Scotland announced new criteria to be used by the Department of Agriculture and Fisheries for Scotland in determining the release of land from agriculture for forestry (Hansard Vol 92: OR Col 353-5W).

James Hunter (1985): *New Opportunities in Farming: A Rural Forum Discussion Paper*
MAFF/DAFS/WOAD/FC (1985): *Woodland as a Farm Crop*
RICS (Scottish Branch) (1985): *Report of Working Party on Farm Forestry*
HIDB (1986): *Farm Woodland Investment Scheme (The IFFI Scheme)*
NCC/Laurence Gould Consultants (1986): *Changes in Land Use in England, Scotland and Wales, 1985-2000* (draft)

3 Forestry and the National Economy

The Nature Conservancy Council has looked beyond the immediate environmental effects of forestry on nature conservation to a broad analysis of the economic rationale for afforestation. Bowers, from Leeds University, produced such an analysis on contract to the Council and this was followed by a comprehensive review by Grove for the British Association of Nature Conservationists. Indicative of the controversy surrounding this subject, Stewart, one of the authors of the 1980 Centre for Agricultural Strategy report on a strategy for the UK forest industry, subsequently gave an alternative view in a 1985 article. Grundy surveyed these economic arguments for the Forestry Commission and the UK Centre for Economic and Environmental Development reviewed and analysed the available data in a major study of forestry policy.

NCC (Bowers) (1983): *The Economics of Upland Land Use: NCC Chief Scientist Team Report, No 538*
BANC (Grove) (1983): *The Future for Forestry.* British Association for Nature Conservationists
Stewart (1985): *British Forest Policy: Time for Change. Land Use Policy, 2 (1): 16-29*
Grundy (1986): *Developing the Economic Arguments for Investment in Forestry: A Survey. Forestry Commission Research and Development Paper 145*
UK CEED (1986): *Forestry: Britain's Growing Resource*

4 Fiscal Support

Dismay has been expressed that the fiscal support structure for forestry encourages institutional and syndicate ownership of forest areas and extensively managed, capital intensive forest systems. The development of the private forestry companies, maximising the advantages of this system as a tax efficient method of building up an appreciating capital asset and the poor support that the tax system is alleged to provide for conservation orientated management has led to a number of studies being undertaken.

Prior (1982): *An Economic Analysis of Silvicultural Options for Broadleaved Woodland. CFI Occasional Paper 19, Volume I Oxford*
Lorrain-Smith (1982): *An Economic Analysis of Silvicultural Options for Broadleaved Woodland. CFI Occasional Paper 19 Vol II Oxford*
Lorrain-Smith (1983): *The Effects of Grants, Taxation and Controls on Broadleaved Woodland Management. NCC*
Roberts (1985): *Forestry as an Investment.* Fountain Forestry
Carroll (1986): *Incentives for Woodland Conservation:* Report Prepared for NCC, CCS and CC(EW)

5 Afforestation and Nature Conservation

The key paper on this subject was the draft of the Nature Conservancy Council's paper, the final version of which has recently been published. The RSPB published their concerns about afforestation of the flow country in Caithness and Sutherland.

NCC (1985): *Afforestation and Nature Conservation in Great Britain* (Draft)
RSPB (1985): *Forestry in the Flow Country – The Threat to Birds*

The Forestry Commission and the Royal Society for the Protection of Birds are carrying out a study on the edge effect of afforestation in Sutherland and Caithness on adjoining wader habitats.

6 Forest Practice and Conservation

There has also been publication of a wide array of advice from a variety of sources on how foresters can improve forests and take into consideration the needs of conservation. Most important in this respect is the TGUK Code of Practice published in November 1985.

Prior (1983): *Trees and Deer.* Batsford, London
Evans (1984): *Silviculture of Broadleaved Woodland. Bulletin 62,* Forestry Commission
TGUK (1985): *The Forestry and Woodland Code*
Smart and Andrews (1985): *Birds and Broadleaves Handbook.* RSPB
Low (1985): *Guide to Upland Restocking Practice. Leaflet 84,* Forestry Commission
Low (1986): *Use of Broadleaved Species in Upland Forests. Leaflet 88,* Forestry Commission

7 Research

The continuing debate about forestry has, inevitably, led to suggestions for further research. In recognition of this the Forestry Research Co-ordination Committee has initiated four review groups with terms of reference which have close relevance to these discussions.

FRCC/Britton (1984): *Research on Integration of Forestry and Farming in the Lowlands*
FRCC/Workman (1985): *Research on Broadleaved Woodland*
FRCC/Hummel: *Research on Forestry and the Environment* — Report yet to be published
FRCC/Cunningham: *Research on Integration of Farming and Forestry in the Uplands* — Report yet to be published

8 Conferences, Seminars and Meetings

In addition to these reports, papers and publications, there have been a large number of conferences, meetings and seminars on aspects of forestry in Scotland. In the six months between the circulation of our discussion paper and our final policy paper being put to the printers, the following conferences have taken place and have played their part in the developing of our thinking.

CCS/FC (November 1985): Broadleaved Woodland in Scotland
ITE/Brathens (December 1985): Trees and Wildlife in the Scottish Uplands
Perth and Kinross District Council (December 1985): Afforestation in Perth and Kinross: Potentials and Conflicts
Environmental Conservation and Development Group (Stirling University) (January 1986): Forestry
Saltire Society (January 1986): The Changing Role for Forestry
Wildlife Link and Countryside Link (February 1986): Forestry Seminar
Royal Institution of Chartered Surveyors (Scottish Branch) (February 1986): Farm Forestry
Scottish Agricultural Colleges (February 1986): The Future of Agriculture in the Hills and Uplands
Scottish Landowners' Federation (March 1986): Tomorrow's Harvest
British Association of Nature Conservationists (March 1986): The Future for Afforestation in the Northern Uplands
Centre for Agricultural Strategy (April 1986): Land Use Alternatives for UK Agriculture

28. Spruce and birch above the River
Tay, Perthshire.